I0083353

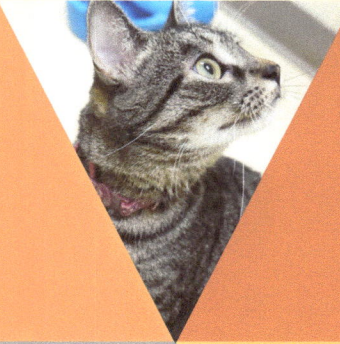

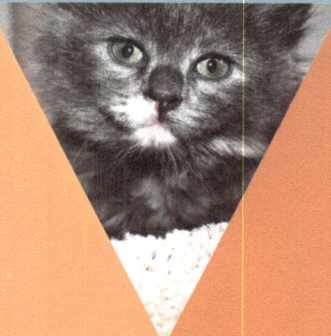

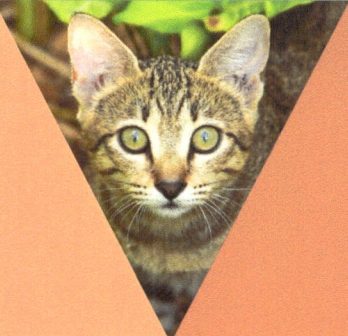

Every Dog's Dream Rescue

A portion of all profits earned from your purchase of this book will be sent to Every Dog's Dream Rescue, Inc., a group of compassionate volunteers working around the clock to provide a safe haven for all the animals that are bought into their rescue facility. Every Dog's Dream not only maintains high-quality care for rescued dogs; they also take in cats and small animals. They operate an adoption center located within the Petco facility on Harry L. Drive in Johnson City, New York, where they always have an abundance of cats and kittens and a number of puppies up for adoption. Every Dog's Dream helps families across New York State to care for stray cats. They also help provide food and veterinary care for those who cannot afford to pay but don't want to give up their animals.

To find out more or to donate, go to: EveryDogsDream.org

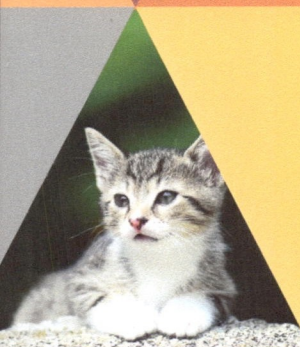

Caring for Cats

Village Earth Press

Copyright © 2017 by Village Earth Press,
a division of Harding House Publishing.

All rights reserved. No part of this
publication may be reproduced or
transmitted in any form or by any means,
electronic or mechanical, including
photocopying, recording, taping, or any
information storage and retrieval system,
without permission from the publisher.

Village Earth Press
Vestal, New York 13850
www.villageearthpress.com

First Printing
9 8 7 6 5 4 3 2 1

ISBN: 978-1-62524-450-5
series ISBN: 978-1-62524-449-9

Author: Rae Simons
Design: Micaela Grace Sanna

Caring for Cats

RAE SIMONS

Village Earth Press

TABLE OF CONTENTS:

Did You Know?

Like your fingerprints, a cat's nose print is one of a kind. No other cat's nose print is just like it.

Introduction

· ·

Animal lives matter. Human welfare and animal welfare are interwoven so tightly that they cannot be separated. In other words, what hurts animals will ultimately hurt us as well.

We can see this at the planetary level. As animals lose their habitats because of climate change, pollution, deforestation, and other factors, human well-being is also threatened. Sometimes, people seem to think it's an either-or situation: we either help people (by investing in businesses that are harming the environment) or we help animals (by hindering the success of those same businesses). That's not the way things work on our planet, though. We are all in this together. What puts animals at risk is an equal risk to human well-being.

We are not only linked to animals at the biological and environmental level. We also share many of the same emotions with them—and how we treat animals can't be separated from how we treat each other. Mark Bekoff, an evolutionary biologist, said in an interview with *Forbes* magazine:

> how we treat other animals has direct effects on how we feel about ourselves …compassion begets compassion.… So, when we're nice to other animals and empathize compassionately with their physical and mental health we're also spreading compassion to other people.

The more scientists learn about animals, the more they find that the creatures with whom we share our planet are far more amazing than we ever knew. Scientists have proven that even fish are conscious and sentient; they've discovered that it's not only our dogs who are sensitive to our pain but that rats, mice, and even chickens are as well; and they also have proof that crows can use tools that are more sophisticated than chimpanzees'. What's more, based on animals' neurochemicals, our furred and feathered friends experience the same feelings of love that humans do.

Earlier cultures thought of animals as our brothers and sisters, but somehow, our culture lost track of that perspective. We need to regain it, not only for animals' sakes but for our own—and we need to teach it to our children. By teaching children how to care for animals (whether pets, farm animals, or wild animals), we are empowering children to become kinder and more responsible.

Psychologists, educators, and other experts agree. The National PTA Congress wrote:

Children trained to extend justice, kindness, and mercy to animals become more just, kind, and considerate in their relations to each other. Character training along these lines will result in men and women of broader sympathies; more humane, more law abiding, in every respect more valuable citizens.

When children learn compassion and respect for animals, they are better able to extend compassion and respect to each other. A relationship with an animal also helps children gain self-confidence; research even indicates that being with an animal helps children relax and learn better. And by speaking out for those who cannot speak for themselves, children learn leadership and the power of their own voices to make the world a better place.

Village Earth Press has created this series of books because we believe that we need to take action on animals' behalf. We also believe that children should have opportunities to become all they can be. Our hope is that this book will contribute to both those goals.

Read more on this topic (and then discuss with children what you learn). We recommend these books:

The Emotional Lives of Animals
by Mark Bekoff

The Ten Trusts: What We Must Do to Care for the Animals We Love
by Jane Goodall

The Pig Who Sang to the Moon: The Emotional World of Farm Animals
by Jeffrey Moussaieff Masson

The Bond: Our Kinship with Animals, Our Call to Defend Them
by Wayne Pacelle

chapter 1

Cats, Cats, Cats Everywhere!

This is an African wildcat. Not all of these cats became domesticated. Today, some of them still exist in the wild.

About 6,000 years ago, a wildcat from the desert slunk into a village in Egypt. She sniffed through the garbage, looking for food. Then she saw something move. A big rat was poking through the garbage too. The cat froze. Her eyes got big. The tip of her tail twitched just a little . . . her muscles got ready to . . . POUNCE! She grabbed the rat with her sharp claws and teeth. With the dead rat in her mouth, she trotted back to her kittens.

In a nearby house, a woman stood in her doorway, watching the cat. She had seen the whole thing. She was glad the rat was dead. Rats were a big nuisance. They got in people's food and ruined it. They carried germs that made people sick. The woman wished she could ask the cat to come back and kill more rats.

Then the woman had an idea. That night she put out a dish of food for the cat. She hoped the cat would come back— and that when the cat found the food, she would want to come back again, looking for more food. So every night the woman put out more food. And sure enough, the cat kept coming back. The cat ate the

Dogs and cats first made friends with humans in similar ways. Wolves and wildcats both started hanging around people in order to get food. But people then trained wolves—dogs—to be better herders, hunters, and watchdogs. People picked out dogs that were especially good at those jobs and made sure those dogs had puppies. People left cats pretty much alone, though. Cats lived with people because they wanted to, not because people made them. Today, dogs have been living with humans for more than 30,000 years, while cats have only been domesticated for about 10,000 years. All this means that house cats are a lot more like wildcats than dogs are like wolves!

scraps the woman left for her, but she also caught more rats. Now there were fewer rats in the woman's house.

The woman told her neighbors about the good idea she'd had. They wanted a cat to come kill their rats too. Soon, everyone in the village was leaving food on the steps of their houses. More and more wildcats came into the village. The cats were glad for the extra food—and the people were glad that the cats were killing the rats.

At first, the wildcats were afraid of people. They ran away whenever someone came near. But little by little, the cats got used to people. They understood that the people weren't going to hurt them. The wildcats decided to live in the village now. They had their kittens there.

The village no longer had a big problem with rats. The villagers were grateful to the cats. They fell in love with the kittens. One day, a little girl found some kittens with no mother. She brought the kittens home with her, and they grew up in her house. They were no longer wild. Now they were tame. And when those cats had kittens, they were tame too. Little by little, cats were **domesticated**.

More and more cats began living in houses with people. People were glad to have them, because they knew the cats would kill rats (and mice too). Cats and people became friends. They learned to love each other.

What's that mean?

DOMESTICATED means that an animal is tame. It lives with people. It's not a wild animal.

The Timeline of Cats

We don't know exactly how cats went from being wild to domesticated. The story at the beginning of this chapter is just make-believe—but we do know that something like that really did happen. To understand more about cats' history, take a look at this timeline.

20 million years ago

The first cat-like animals appear on the Earth. They're called miacids.

12 million years ago

The oldest known relative of today's domestic cat comes into being. Their closest relative today is the European wildcat.

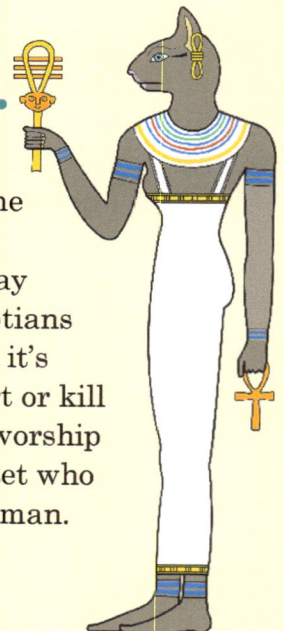

4000 BCE

In ancient Egypt, the African wildcat enters towns in search of food and chooses to live close to people.

2000 BCE

The Egyptians welcome cats into their homes because they keep away rats and snakes. Egyptians like cats so much that it's against the law to hurt or kill a cat. Egyptians also worship a goddess named Bastet who is half cat and half woman.

1000 BCE–500 BCE

It's against the law to take cats out of Egypt, but traders sneak them out secretly. Domesticated cats spread across Southeast Asia, into India, and then into Rome, in what is now Italy.

500 CE

The Roman Empire gets bigger, and cats spread throughout all the Empire's land, across Europe and into Britain.

1400s

People blame the Devil for the Black Death that spreads across Europe, killing thousands of people. Women are killed for being witches, in league with the Devil, and cats are killed for being the "Devil's pet."

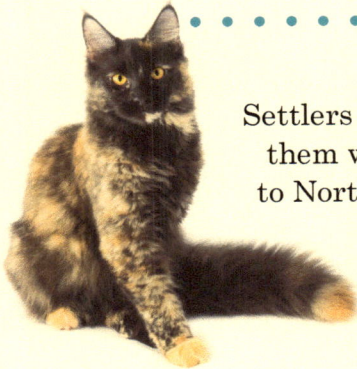

1500s

Cats are kept on ships to kill rats. When explorers come across the Atlantic Ocean, they bring cats with them. Cats' sense of balance makes them do well on ships.

1700s

Settlers bring cats with them when they come to North America. The domestic cat then spreads across North and South America.

1800s

The popularity of cats as pets grows, but many people are still cruel to cats. In 1871, the first cat show takes place in London.

1914–1918

During World War I, cats are used to sniff out poisonous gas and on warships to control rats.

1990s

Around the world, cats become more popular as pets than dogs.

2000s

Cats are everywhere! They come in different breeds, different colors, and different sizes. But they're all wonderful.

Today, the most popular furry pet in America is the cat. Cats come in many different colors and sizes. Some have long hair, some have short hair. Some cats have hardly any hair at all! Some cats still kill mice and rats. But others just lie around and sleep. They play with toys. They sit on their owners' laps and purr. They make people feel happier just by being around them. Other cats go to shows. They win prizes for looking pretty.

Long-hair and short-hair. Blue eyes and green eyes. Fancy and ordinary. Noisy and quiet. Big and small. Lively and sleepy. There are all kinds of cats. No cat is quite like any other. Each one is special. There are nearly 100 million pet cats just in the United States (and a lot more in other parts of the world). That's a lot of cats!

There are lots of different cat breeds. Here are some of the most common.

Sphynx

The hairless sphynx isn't completely hairless. These cats have soft fuzz all over their bodies. They can't live outside because they can get sunburned. They get cold easily. They like to snuggle and cuddle.

Siamese

Siamese kitties have blue eyes. They like to "talk." They're intelligent and affectionate. They get lonely if they can't be with their owners.

Abyssinian

This is one of the oldest cat breeds. It's closest to the African wildcats. These cats love to play with water. They love their families, but they are shy around strangers.

Maine Coon

Maine Coon cats are the largest domesticated cats. They're taller, longer, and heavier than most other cats. They're good-natured and gentle, though.

Bengal

Bengal cats are actually part Asian leopard. Back in the 1950s, an ordinary house cat and a leopard had kittens, and that was the beginning of this type of cat. They are completely domesticated now, and their intelligence makes them interesting pets who love to play games.

American Shorthairs

These cats are the great-great-great-(many-more-times-great)-grandchildren of the first cats to come to the United States. They started out as working cats that were expected to kill rats and mice, but today they are the most common domesticated cat in the United States.

Persian

Persian cats are pretty, but their long hair does take care. They do best living indoors. They're gentle and sweet.

What's that mean?

To SCAVENGE means to look for food, often in garbage or places where no one else wants anything.

But not all cats have homes. Some cats live in rescue shelters. Others live on their own. They **scavenge** for their food, the way the African wildcats did thousands of years ago. They don't have anyone to feed them. They don't have anyone to take care of them if they get sick.

Some homeless cats are used to people. They're friendly and would love to have a home where someone would love them and take care of them. Other homeless cats, however, have gone back to being wild. They're scared of people. They may scratch and bite to protect themselves if someone tries to touch them.

Did You Know?

There are over 500 million domesticated cats living in the world.

Cats in shelters have a safe place to sleep. They have someone to feed them and make sure they're healthy. But they miss having a home of their own. They miss having their own family to love them.

There are so many homeless cats in the world, that if your family has decided to get a cat, you should think about getting one from a shelter. You could give a home to a homeless cat or kitten who needs one. You could make sure that cat was safe and healthy and loved.

Deciding to have a cat is a big decision. You have to think about it. You can't just get a cat because you think it's cute. You need to know ahead of time what a cat will need. You want to be sure you can give your cat what he needs to be happy and healthy. You need to be ready to do your part!

2

Adopting a Cat or Kitten

Kittens are cute. They love to play, and they can be a lot of fun. They also love people. When they grow up, they will love the people who care for them. Cats and humans have been good friends for hundreds of years. Curling up with a purring kitty is a nice, cozy feeling.

But cats aren't toys! They are living creatures. They need care and attention, just like you do. They can also be a lot of work. You and your family need to think carefully before you decide to get a kitten or a cat. There are lots of things to think about.

First of all, is your home a good place for a cat? Cats don't need as much room as a dog does, but they do need places where they will feel safe. Kittens and younger cats like to run around and play. Does your family's house or apartment have room for a cat to do that?

Some cats go outside whenever they want. Cats love to explore the outdoors, but they may not be safe out there.

Cats can turn almost anything into a toy. Even toilet paper!

Cats who live indoors often live longer than cats that go outdoors. Dogs and wild animals can be dangerous to cats. Your pet might also catch diseases from other cats. She could be hit by a car.

If you have an indoor cat, you will need to have a cat box. Cats go to the bathroom in a box filled with kitty litter. They make their pee and their poop in the box. You can't flush a cat box the way you do the toilet, though. That means the litter needs to be changed often. If it isn't, pretty soon your home will smell bad. So if you're thinking about getting a cat, make sure someone will be willing to take care of the cat box. That person could be you! It's not a hard job, but it does need to be done often.

There are other things to think about before you get a cat. How do the other people in your family feel about cats? You need to be sure everyone who lives in your home will welcome a cat. Sometimes people feel nervous or uncomfortable around cats. Some people are allergic to cats. This means that being around cats makes them feel sick. They might not be able to

Cats like to crawl inside things. They are very curious, and they like to explore.

Sometimes older cats can be very gentle with young children, and young children can learn to be gentle with cats. But you need to be careful when little kids and cats are together, because they might hurt each other.

breathe very well if a cat is anywhere near them. If someone in your house is allergic to cats, then your family shouldn't get one.

Here's something else you should think about—are there little kids in your home? Very young children don't always understand that cats and kittens need to be handled gently. They could squeeze the cat too tight or pull his tail. If they scare the cat, he might scratch them. So if you have younger brothers and sisters, you might need to wait until they're a little older before you get a kitten or cat.

Another thing to think about is whether the pets you already have in your home will get along with a new cat. Pets usually need time to get used to each other, but some dogs and cats can become good friends. Other dogs may not understand that the cat is a member of the family. They might hurt or even kill the cat. You need to be sure that any pets you have will be able to accept a new animal in the house. If you have small pets, like birds or hamsters, you will also need to make sure that they would be safe from a cat. Most cats won't understand that your little pets are important to you. Cats who live in the wild catch birds and small animals for their dinner, and house cats still have those same instincts. You need to

A dog and cat who grow up together will usually be good friends their whole lives. This dog isn't trying to eat the cat! He's actually playing with the cat, and he's being very careful not to use his teeth. The cat isn't worried. She trusts her friend not to hurt her.

What's that mean?

An INSTINCT is something an animal does without thinking about it. Birds who fly south in the winter do so because of their instincts. Mother animals take care of their babies because of instinct. People have instincts too, but we also can think about and control what we do more than animals can.

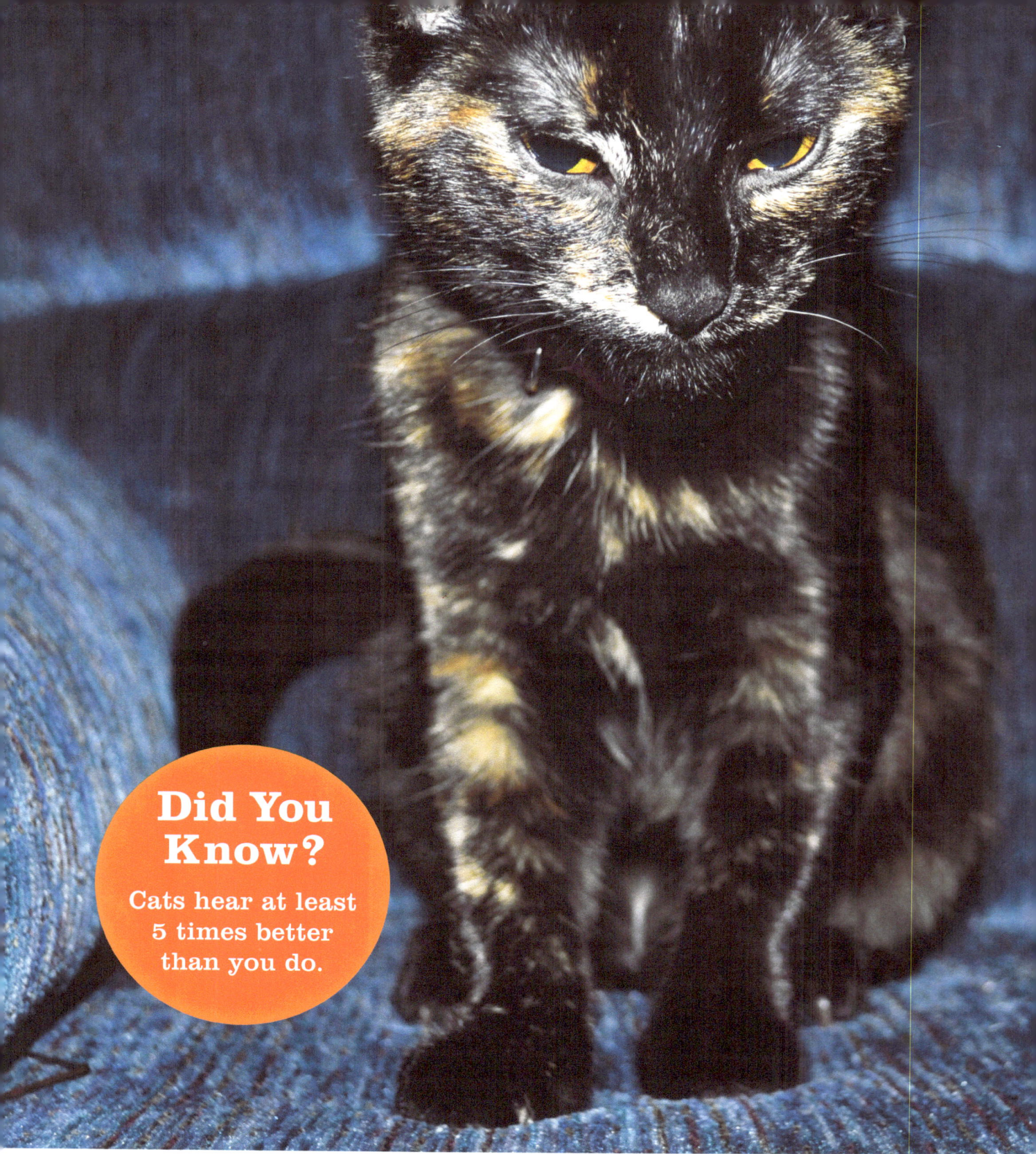

Did You Know?

Cats hear at least 5 times better than you do.

make sure that none of your pets can hurt each other!

You also need to think about the kind of furniture in your house. Cats have sharp claws, and they need to sharpen them on something. They need a place where it's okay for them to scratch. Kittens can be taught where they should and shouldn't sharpen their claws. While they're learning, though, they might damage sofas and carpets. Kittens could also have an accident on floors or furniture. They'll learn to use their litter box, but until they do, they could pee somewhere they're not supposed to. If there are very expensive carpets and furniture in your home, it might not be a good place for a kitten. An older cat who already knows how to behave might be a better choice for your family.

Before you bring a cat or kitten home, make sure you have food and dishes ready for your new pet. Cats need to be fed every day. Cat food doesn't cost a lot, but make sure the grown-ups in your house don't mind paying for it. Cats also need to have fresh, clean water to drink. If you're going to have a cat, you have to take care of her every day. You can't forget some days. Imagine how you would feel if your family forgot to buy groceries or put meals on the table every day. Cats can't go to the refrigerator and get their own food. They can't go to the sink

Kittens sold at pet stores could have come from a "kitten mill," a place that has lots of mother cats making lots of kittens. The cats often live their whole lives in cages, and their kittens can have health problems.

What's that mean?

A RESPONSIBILITY is something you have to do, even when you don't feel like doing it. It's a job that people count on you to do.

A VETERINARIAN is a doctor who takes care of animals. Lots of times, people call this kind of doctor a VET for short.

and get a drink of water when they're thirsty. They count on the people in their lives to do that for them. Are you ready for that **responsibility**?

Cats need to go to a **veterinarian** at least once a year, just like you need to go to a doctor for checkups. Cats and kittens also need shots to stay healthy,

If you get a new cat or kitten, you should take him to see a vet. The vet will check him over to make sure he is healthy. The kitten will also need shots that will keep him from getting sick. Veterinarian bills can be expensive, so make sure your family is ready to pay for the care a cat needs.

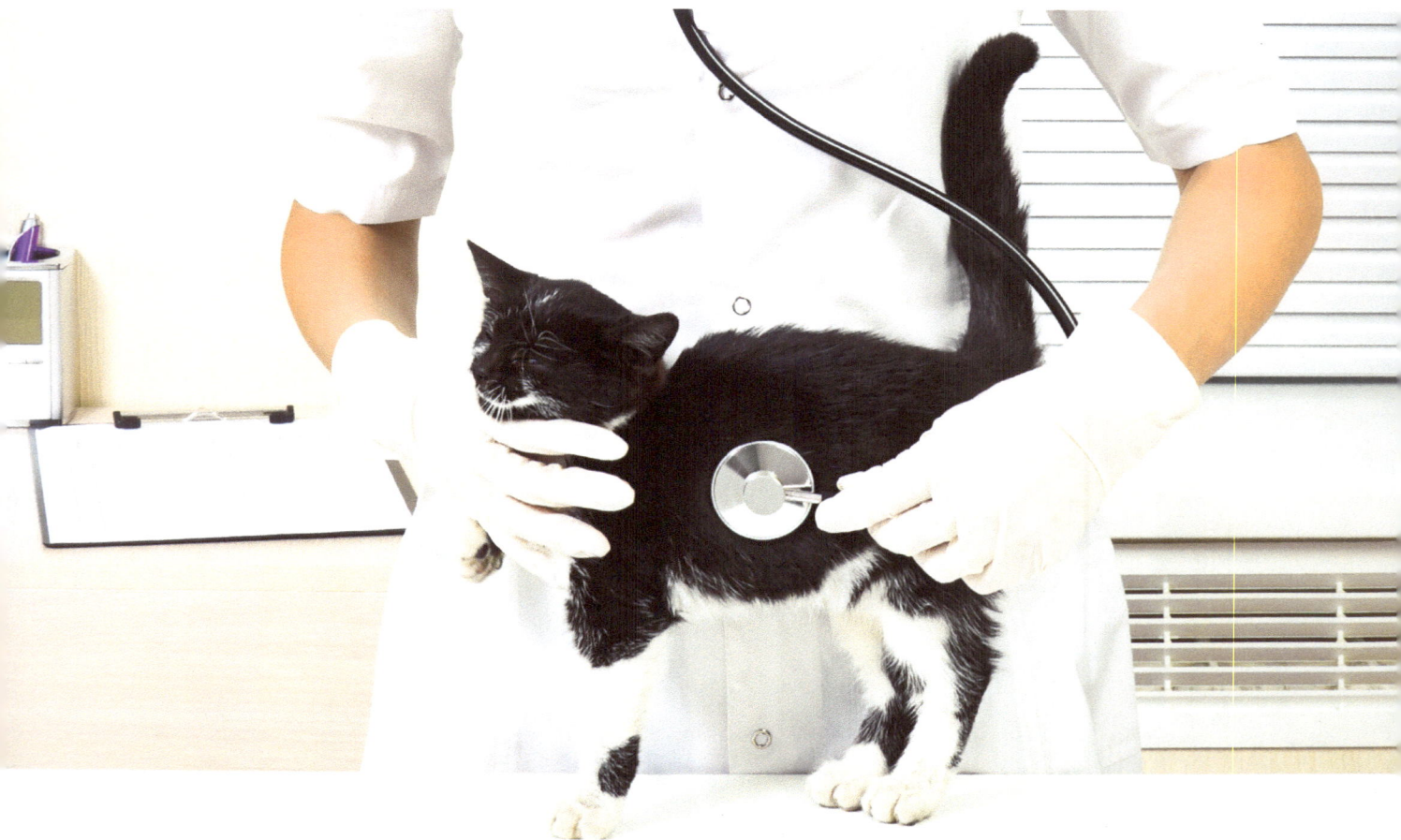

the same way you do. Cats don't get sick very often, but if they do, they need to see a veterinarian. They might need medicine to help them get better. Cats can get fleas, little bugs that make cats—and people!—very itchy. A vet will be able to help you make sure your cat never gets fleas. If she does get fleas, the vet can help you get rid of them.

Unless your family wants to have kittens, if you have a girl cat, she should have an operation that will keep her from having babies. If you have a boy cat, the vet will give him another sort of operation, so that he can't make a girl cat have kittens. The operation that girl cats get is called "spaying," and the operation that boy cats get is called "neutering."

Most of all, cats need lots of love and attention. If your family is very busy or if you go away from home a lot, then you might not be ready to get a cat. Cats who are left alone too much get lonely. They might get in mischief. They will feel sad and bored, the same way you do when you're alone too long. If you want to get a cat, be ready to pay attention to him every day!

Most cats love to be stroked gently. They like to be with the people they love.

Things you'll need before you bring home a cat:

Cat Box and Kitty Litter

If you scoop out the lumps every day, you won't need to put new litter in the box as often. Be sure to wash your hands when you're done.

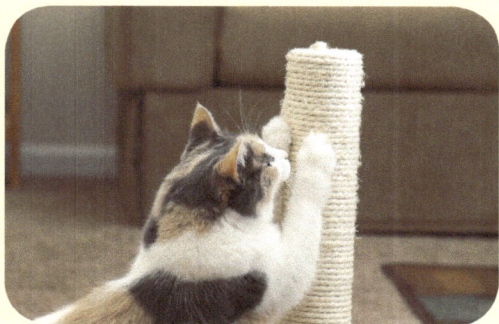

Scratching Post

Cats can learn to sharpen their claws on a scratching post like this instead of on furniture or carpets.

Carrier Crate

If you need to take your cat somewhere in the car, she should ride in a box like this.

Cat Food

Cats eat dry food like this, but they can also have food that comes in a can.

Food and Water Dishes

A cat needs both food and water every day. His water bowl should always have water in it, so he can get a drink whenever he wants.

Cat Toys

Cats love to play. They don't HAVE to have special cat toys like this one, but they need something! They're just as happy to play with a button tied to a piece of string, a spool, or a little ball.

Here are things you don't HAVE to have if you are getting a cat—but they're nice to have:

Cat Bed

Cats love beds that make them feel like they're hiding someplace safe. Cats will find their own places to curl up, though, and they're just as happy with a cardboard box— so you don't HAVE to buy your cat a bed.

Collar and Tag

If your cat never goes outside, she probably doesn't need a collar and tag. But if there's any chance she'll be on her own outdoors, she should have a collar with a tag that has your name, address, and phone number. That way if she gets lost, whoever finds her can bring her back home.

Brush

You can buy a special brush at a pet store that's made just for cats. If your cat has long hair, you'll need to brush him to keep him from getting snarls. Brushing can also keep your cat from shedding so much fur on furniture and other places. Some cats love to be brushed!

Claw Clipper

Clipping your cats claws will keep them from getting too long and sharp. You can use a special cat clipper like this one, but regular nail clippers work just as well. This is probably a job for a grown-up, though, because you have to be careful not to cut too much, which could make the cat bleed.

Spray Cleaner

It's a good idea to have cleaner on hand to take care of any messes your cat makes. Pet stores sell cleaner that's made especially to clean up cat pee and throw-up.

Perch

Cats love to sit up high above the rest of the world. That's why they like to climb trees. Indoor cats can't climb trees, but they love having a perch where they can sit and look down. They also enjoy climbing to get up to the perch, and they can sharpen their claws on it as well.

If you and your family have thought carefully about getting a cat, and you've decided that's what you want to do, what comes next? Where do you find your new cat or kitten?

There are a few places to look. You could go to a pet store, but there are better choices. People who are looking to find a home for their cat or kittens often place an advertisement in the newspaper or on Craigslist. These pets are sometimes free, so long as you can offer a good home. An even better

Kitten or Adult Cat?

Kittens are awfully cute, and they're a lot of fun—but you should also think about adopting an adult cat. The people at the shelter will be able to tell you if an adult cat is already trained to use a litter box, and if the cat is used to being around dogs, children, or other cats and pets. They will be able to tell you a little bit about what the cat is like. Does she like to play—or is she calm and sleepy a lot of the time? Does she love to be with people—or is she happy to be alone sometimes? Is she gentle with children— or does she like to use her claws when she plays? These are all good things to know. But there's also another good reason to adopt an older cat. Most people who want a cat want to start out with a kitten, so kittens in shelters find homes fast. An older cat, however, may NEVER find a home—unless you give him one!

Black cats don't get adopted as much as other cats. Maybe people think they're bad luck. But black cats are just as loving and cute as any other cat. If you're adopting a cat, think about picking a black one that other people may not want!

Every Dog's Dream is a rescue shelter that works with Petco to help both cats and dogs. They take in cats that no one wants, and then they find homes for them. This cat is waiting for a good home.

What's that mean?

A **MIXED-BREED** cat had parents that looked different from each other. Most cats are mixed breed. A **PUREBRED** is a type of cat that looks a certain way. People have made sure that only the same kinds of mother and father cats have had kittens together. Siamese cats, Persian cats, and Sphynx cats are all different types of purebreds.

way to get a new pet, though, is to go a shelter or rescue center. These are places that take in cats or kittens that don't have homes. You'll know exactly what you're getting if you choose your new cat from a shelter.

Shelters are filled with healthy cats and kittens of every color, shape, and size. Most are **mixed-breed** cats, but you can find **purebreds** there too, especially adult purebreds. By adopting one of these cats, you're giving a home to an animal that needs one very much.

At the same time, all the animals in a good shelter have been checked by a vet, so you won't be bringing home a new pet that's sick. Shelters often will spay and neuter their cats too, so you don't have to worry about doing that. They also give cats and kittens the shots they need. The only money you will need to pay will be to cover the cost of shots and spaying or neutering. Adopting a cat from a shelter is a good decision.

3 chapter

Keeping Your Cat Healthy

Do you know what you need to be healthy and happy? You need to eat healthy food. You need to exercise. You need to take baths and stay clean. Sometimes you need to go to the doctor and get shots that will keep you from getting sick. If you do get sick, you may need to go to the doctor for medicine. You need to be able to have fun and do interesting things. You also need people who love you and take care of you.

Your cat needs all those things too. She is counting on you to give her those things. Here are some ways you can give your cat what she needs to be happy and healthy.

Find a good veterinarian.

One of the most important things you can do for your cat is to find a good vet as soon as you bring your cat home. Most vets will see cats, but call first to make sure. Find a vet you trust. She can be a big help to you as you learn to care for you cat. She can work with you to make sure your cat is healthy.

Your cat will probably be scared when she has a checkup at the vet's office. She will feel better if you are with her.

Brush your cat several times a week.

Cats are always licking themselves, so it may seem like they don't need to be brushed too. When a cat licks himself, though, he often swallows fur. That fur can turn into a ball inside him. It can block up the tubes where his food is **digested**. If you brush your cat, though, the loose fur will come out in the brush. Then when he licks himself, he won't be swallowing as much fur. He won't get hairballs.

Many cats like to be brushed. If your cat doesn't like the brush, though, try giving him a treat every time you get out the brush. That way he'll think

What's that mean?

When food is DIGESTED, it is broken down inside your body so that your body can use it for staying alive and healthy.

of treats whenever you brush him—and that will make him like being brushed.

Feed your cat healthy food.

If you walk down the pet food aisle at the grocery store, you'll find many, many kinds of cat food. Some of it is in cans, and some is in bags. Some costs more than others. How do you know which kind is best for your cat?

Veterinarians say that usually canned food is better than dry. Cats need lots of protein and lots of water, and canned food has more of both. Dry food is less expensive, though. You could give your cat some of both dry and wet food each day. If you give her only dry food, though, you need to be sure that she doesn't eat too much. If you give your cat big bowls of dry food every day, she could get fat. It's not healthy for cats to have too much fat, so make sure you only give her the amount of food she really needs. If you only feed your cat dry food, you also need to be sure she is drinking a lot of fresh water. If she doesn't, she could get sick.

You can talk to your vet to find out how much food you should be giving your cat. Different cats need different amounts of food. They may need different kinds of food too. Kittens need different food from adult cats, and they need to eat more often. If your cat is sick, he may need special food. Your vet can tell you exactly what your cat needs.

Some cats are fussy about what they like to eat. If you have a finicky kitty, she may like canned food better than dry. Or she may only like one brand of food and refuse to eat anything else. She could like only new brands of food, and then get tired of them once she's used to them. Cats are like people—every one is different. Pay attention

to what your cat likes and doesn't like. Once you get to know her, you will understand what she likes to eat. Always check with your vet, though, to make sure her **diet** is healthy.

Don't give your cat too much people food. Things that are good for people to eat may not be good for your kitty. Here are some things that you shouldn't let your cat eat:

- bones
- food that has onion, garlic, or tomato in it
- chocolate
- fatty foods

Some table scraps won't hurt your cat—but you don't want him to get so used to eating people food that he doesn't want to eat cat food! These foods are okay to give your cat as a treat once in a while:

- plain yogurt
- cheese
- a little butter (It helps any hairballs he might have to slide out of the tubes inside him.)
- cooked chicken or turkey
- canned fish
- cooked eggs

Make sure your cat always has a bowl of clean, fresh water.

Long, long ago, the first cats lived in the desert. There wasn't a lot of drinking water there, so cats got most of their water from the bodies of the animals they caught and ate. A mouse is nearly three-quarters water! Today, most cats don't eat mice. This means they need to get their water from a bowl—and they need YOU to keep that bowl always full.

What's that mean?

DIET is what a cat (or a person) usually eats.

Always use a carrier when you take your cat to the vet. The carrier will keep your cat from running away—and it will also keep him safe from any other animals that might be at the vet's office.

Spay or neuter your cat.

When a girl cat is spayed, that means the vet does an operation so she can't have babies. When a boy cat is neutered, he can't make a girl cat have babies. There are a few good reasons to do this. Girl cats that aren't spayed, will go into "heat" every few weeks. During this time, they could get pregnant from a boy cat. Girl cats aren't happy when they are in heat. It feels uncomfortable. They may cry

After a girl cat is spayed, she will have a line of stitches on her belly. Don't pet them or pick at them. If you see the skin around the stitches look red and puffy, let your vet know right away. Your cat may have gotten an infection, and your vet will need to give her medicine to help her heal. Usually, the stitches will fall out by themselves. Your cat's fur will grow back, and she will be as good as new.

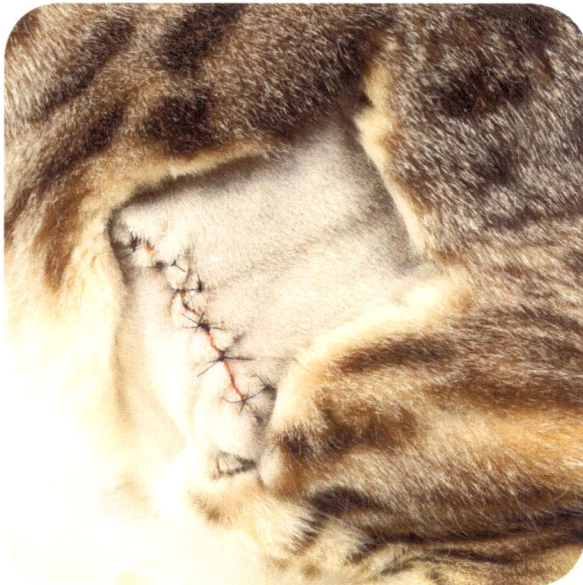

a lot. They may also cry very loudly, until you get tired of hearing them! Boy cats that haven't been neutered will want to get outside and wander away from home. They may get in fights with other boy cats, and they could get seriously hurt. Both boy and girl cats are happier when they have the operations they need. Another good reason for making sure cats are spayed or neutered is that there are already more kittens in the world than people want. Those kittens don't have homes or people to love them. You don't want your cat to add to the problem by making more kittens.

Most kittens are spayed or neutered when they are two or three months old. If you got your cat from a shelter, the cat may have already been spayed or neutered. Your vet will be able to tell you when and if your cat needs this operation. If she does, the vet will make an appointment for you to bring your cat to his office. You'll leave your cat there. While you're gone, the vet will give your cat a shot that makes her go to sleep. Then the vet will shave a little fur off from her belly and make a cut in the cat's skin. He will cut an inside part that will keep her from having babies, and then he will sew her up. Once she is awake, you can come and take her home. She will be sore, so she will need you to take care extra good care of her. Don't play roughly with her. Make sure she has a soft quiet place to sleep. Soon she will be back to normal.

Keep your cat safe in the car.

When you ride in the car, you wear a seatbelt. The seatbelt keeps you from getting hurt if the car has to stop suddenly. Cats can't wear seatbelts, though. That's why they should always travel inside a carrier. The carrier will keep them from flying around the car and getting hurt if there's an accident. It will also keep them from CAUSING an accident by bothering the driver.

Never leave your cat alone in the car for more than a few minutes. Even if you're only going to be gone for a little while, make sure the windows are rolled down an inch or two and the car is parked in the shade. A stopped car can become too hot for a cat very quickly. When that happens, the cat can die.

Some cats like to go for rides in the car, but others hate it. Whether your cat loves it or hates it, it's a good idea to leave him home unless he's going somewhere he needs to go (like the vet's).

Keep your cats from eating poisonous plants.

Some houseplants are poisonous to kitties. To be safe, make sure all the plants in your house are placed somewhere your cat can't nibble on them. If you think your cat may have eaten something she shouldn't, call your vet right away.

Keep your cat from getting fleas and worms.

When you first get a cat, take him to the vet as soon as possible. The vet will make sure he doesn't have fleas or worms—and if he does, your vet will give him medicine that kills the fleas and worms. Worms can make your cat sick, and you don't want him to be itchy from fleabites. You don't want to have fleabites either! If your cat goes outside or is around other cats, he may need something to keep him from getting fleas or worms. Talk to your vet. She will be able to tell you what your cat needs.

Make sure your cat gets exercise.

Cats need to have room to run around and play. Younger cats need more exercise than older cats, but all cats need to be able to move around. Don't keep them cooped up in a small space, or they will be sad, sick, and bored.

Make sure your cat gets plenty of attention.

Cats get lonely, just like people do. A cat can stay alone at home while you're away for a little while—but not too long or very often. Cats need to be with the people they love (just like you do).

Taking care of a cat is a big job. But it's worth it. And you can do it! You can give your cat what he needs to be happy and healthy.

chapter 4

Understanding Your Cat

Did you know that cats have their own language? They talk with their voices, and they talk with their bodies. They use their tail, their ears, their eyes, and even their fur to give you messages. And of course they also purr!

Cats speak a different language from dogs. For example, when a dog wags his tail, he's usually feeling friendly. But when a cat's tail goes back and forth, she's usually mad. Cats have lots of different moods, and that's different from dogs too. Dogs also have feelings, of course, but a lot of the time, they're pretty happy. They're almost always ready to play. A cat doesn't always feel like playing. She doesn't always want to be pet either. Sometimes she wants to be left alone. She can't use words to tell you when you're bugging her, so she uses her body.

Your cat wants to tell you what he wants and how he feels. He wants to let you know if he's in a good mood or if he's feeling grumpy. If you learn to understand "cat language," you'll be able to take care of your cat better. Understanding his language will help you be good friends who trust each other.

Here is a key to your cat's moods:

When your cat is sitting or lying down, with his eyes half-closed and his pupils narrow, he's feeling happy. If he's feeling pleased about something, he'll also purr.

If your cat looks at you and slowly blinks her eyes, it's her way of giving you a kiss.

A cat who is happy to see someone will rub against the person's legs. He may be saying, "Welcome home!" Or he might be saying, "Finally! You're feeding me!"

When your cat has her ears forward and her head outstretched, she is interested in something. She's feeling curious!

When a cat crouches down with his eyes wide and his tail twitching back and forth, he's getting ready to pounce on something. Cats catch mice like this—but they also play with toys the same way. Sometimes they like to play with people's feet too!

When your cat puts her ears back, she's feeling a little grumpy. This probably isn't a good time to pet her. She's telling you, "Leave me alone!"

A cat who walks toward you with his tail straight up in the air is happy to see you.

When your cat is feeling worried or upset, she'll tuck her tail between her legs, and walk very close to the floor. Her pupils will be wide, and her ears sideways or back. She needs someplace to hide where she can feel safe.

A cat who pushes his feet up and down on a bed or something soft, is feeling very happy. The soft bed reminds him of the way he felt when he was a kitten with his mother. (This is what kittens do to the mother cat to make her milk come out.)

When your cat is startled or very scared, her fur will puff up along her back and on her tail. She'll push her back up in an arch.

A cat who is enjoying having someone pet her may close her eyes and push her head against the person's hand. She's saying, "That feels good!"

When a cat is completely relaxed, he might lie on his back, with his tummy showing and his legs up. He's not worried about anything. He might also do this when he's playing.

An angry or very scared cat might show his teeth and make a hissing sound. His ears will be almost flat against his head, and he may also growl or yowl.

If your cat butts her head against you, she's saying "I love you!"

Did You Know?

Cats purr because they're happy, but they also purr for other reasons. Scientists think that sometimes cats purr to help themselves heal after they've been hurt.

Did You Know?

Cats can make about 100 different sounds. Dogs can only make about 10.

Dogs and cats may not speak the same language—but that doesn't mean they can't learn to be friends! Dogs and cats are natural enemies, and some dogs and some cats will never get along with each other. Other cats and dogs, though, can learn to love each other, especially if they've grown up together.

Cats also use their voices to talk to you. Some cats talk more than others. Siamese cats, for example, have a lot to say! "Meow," can mean a lot of things. It might mean, "I'm lonely. Pay attention to me!" It could mean, "I'm hungry!" A loud yowl might mean, "I'm angry. Leave me alone!" It could mean, "Help! I'm stuck in the closet! Let me out!" It might also mean, "I feel sick! Something hurts!" Cats can make chirping noises too. When your cat sees you when you come home after school, she might make a little chirp and run toward you. She's saying, "Hello! I'm happy to see you!" A cat who is watching birds or squirrels outside the window might make a chittery-chattery noise. She's probably saying to the birds, "I wish I could get out and catch you!"

Dogs and cats are different from each other in another way. Dogs usually like new experiences. They like to go to new places with their owners. Cats don't. They like things to stay the same most of the time. If there are too many new things in their life, cats feel stressed and unhappy.

Here are some things that could stress your cat:

- Moving to a new house.
- Having a new person or animal in the house.
- Moving his bed.
- Moving your furniture around.
- Loud noises.
- A strange cat hanging around outside.
- Your family going on vacation and leaving him alone.
- A change in your family's routine. For instance, your cat may feel unhappy when you go back to school in the fall.
- When you or someone in your house is upset. Cats are good at picking up peoples' feelings. If you feel stressed, your cat probably will too. And if your family is arguing and fighting a lot, your cat could feel worried and upset.

When something is making your cat feel worried, he might hide and not come out. He might not want to eat. He might also do things he's not supposed to, like peeing where he shouldn't.

There are things you can do to help your cat if she's feeling upset:

- Make sure she has someplace safe to hide until she's feeling better. You could make her a bed in a closet, behind a sofa, or under a bed.

- Play with her. Exercise will help her be able to relax later.
- Give her something new to play with. Cats don't like big changes in their lives—but they do like new toys. You don't always have to buy cat toys at the store either. Cats love empty paper bags and boxes. They like crinkly, crackly things. They like to play with twist-ties and bottle caps. A walnut or a ball of aluminum foil makes a good toy too, and so does anything that dangles from a string.
- Give her a place where she can sit up high. You can buy a "cat tree," but you could also give your cat a safe place to sit on top of a bookshelf.
- Find a windowsill where she can look out. Cats love to watch what's going on outside.

Sometimes cats do things you don't want them to do—like scratching furniture or peeing on the carpet. Always remember that your cat's not "bad" when he does these

Wild cats go up into trees where they can watch the world. Your cat will enjoy having a place where he can do the same thing. He feels safe when he's up high, and he'll like to watch what's going on from up there.

Give your cat a scratching post that's sturdy and about three feet high. Cats like to stretch when they scratch, so you want a post that's tall enough and won't fall over.

things. Yelling at him won't help much, especially if he doesn't really understand why you're yelling. Never ever hit your cat or kick him! Instead, if you understand why your cat is acting the way he is, you can help him act differently.

All cats need to "sharpen their claws." They're not really making their claws sharper, though. Scratching their claws on something gets rid of the dead layer that's on the outside of their claws. It's a little like when you cut your fingernails. They don't mean to ruin your furniture or carpets. They're just doing what comes naturally to them.

Some people have their cats declawed to stop them from scratching things. This is a very mean thing to do to a cat. When a cat is declawed, it's not just the claw that's taken out. The first joint of each toe is also cut off. Imagine if someone cut off the tips of all your fingers! Cats who have been declawed can get infections in the wounds. When their paws heal, they can have scars that make it hard for them to walk. A cat that doesn't have claws won't be able to protect herself if she's attacked by a dog or another cat. If she's outside, she won't be able to escape danger by climbing a tree.

A much better answer to your cat's scratching problem is to teach him where it's okay to scratch. A good post has rope wrapped around it. Don't get one that's covered with carpet, because you want to teach your cat that rugs are NOT where he should scratch. Put

the post where he can see it easily. If he's already got a bad habit of scratching something he shouldn't, put the post near to that place.

Here are some ways to get your cat to use the scratching post:

- Rub catnip on the post. (You can buy catnip at a pet store. You might also find it growing wild outdoors.)
- Play with your cat around the post. You might want to tie a toy attached to string to the top of the post.
- Show your cat what to do by pretending to use the post yourself. You might feel silly—but cats are good at copying things they see someone else do.
- Praise your cat and give him a treat whenever he uses the post.

While you're teaching your cat where she SHOULD scratch, you can also teach her to stop scratching where she SHOULDN'T. Here are some ways to do that:

- Put double-sided tape on furniture or carpets where you want your cat to stop scratching. Your cat won't like the sticky tape.
- Tape bubble wrap to furniture arms or drape it over furniture and carpets. If your cat sticks her claws into the bubbles, she won't like the POP! POP!
- Spray a smell that cats don't like wherever you don't want her to

scratch. You can buy this at a pet store, but many cats also don't like the smell of oranges and lemons.

Another problem is when cats don't use their litter boxes. No one wants to live in a house that smells like cat pee! Unlike dogs that have to be taught not to pee and poop on the floor, cats naturally want to use a litter box. Little kittens just need to be shown where to go—and then they will! So if your cat's not using his litter box, there's something wrong. Here are some things you can do:

- Make sure your cat has been neutered or spayed. Cats who haven't been are more likely to want to "mark" things with their pee.
- Make sure your cat isn't sick. Take him to the vet. Cats who have an infection in their **bladders** often pee places where they shouldn't.
- Is the box big enough for your cat? It should be at least as long as he is, and it should be wide enough for him to turn around in it.
- Make sure the sides of the box are low enough for your cat to get in and out easily. This is important for little kittens and also for older cats who may have a hard time stepping over something.
- Use about 2 or 3 inches of litter in the box if your cat is an adult. If he's a kitten, the litter should only be about an inch and a half deep. Cats don't like litter that's too deep.

What's that mean?

A BLADDER is the place inside a cat where her pee is before it comes out. You have a bladder inside you too.

Cats love to sleep. They spend about three-quarters of their time sleeping.

- Don't use a liner on the box. Start out with a box that doesn't have a cover. Later, if you know your cat is always using his box, you could switch to the kind that has a cover—but if he stops using his box, take the cover off!

- Find a litter your cat likes by experimenting with different brands. Once you've found one, stick with it. Cats don't like to have a new kind of litter show up in their box.

- Are you keeping the litter box clean? Cats don't like to use a dirty box. You should take out the clumps once or twice a day. Every couple of weeks, you should empty out all the litter and clean the box with warm, soapy water.

- Put the box somewhere in a corner where your cat will feel safe. It shouldn't be near something that makes a noise like the washing machine or dryer.

- Put a litter box on every level of your house, upstairs and downstairs.

- If you have more than one cat, you should always have as many boxes as you do cats.

Humans sometimes say hello by shaking hands or waving—but animals, including dogs and cats, say hello to each other by touching noses.

There are also ways you can stop your cat from peeing or pooping in places where she shouldn't:

- Make sure you completely clean any place where she's peed or pooped. Baking soda, vinegar, and hydrogen peroxide are good ways to get out the smell. The smell tells your cat it's okay to pee there, so you want to take the smell away.

- Use double-sided tape, bubble wrap, or orange and lemon juice to keep your cat away from the area where she's been peeing or pooping.

- Don't leave clothes lying on the floor. Your cat may think your dirty clothes are a good a place to pee, so keep your room picked up!

- Do the things we talked about earlier to help your cat not feel stressed or upset.

Pay attention to your cat's moods. Learn to speak "cat language." Then you'll be able to understand your cat better.

Remember, though, every cat is different. Some cats are very friendly. Some like to be alone more. Some love to play, and some don't. Your cat won't be just like any other cat, the same way you're not exactly like anyone else. That's why you need to get to know YOUR cat.

When you love someone, you pay attention to that person. You do your best to understand her. If she's sad, you do what you can to help her feel better. When you love your cat, you do all these things too. Your cat needs your love. He needs YOU!

Image Credits

Cover: Elya Vatel (Shutterstock), Evgeniya Pashkova (Dreamstime), Micaela Grace Sanna, Rasa Razaniene (Dreamstime)

Pages 1–4: Alinam119 (Dreamstime), Andreas Hollerer (Dreamstime), Chloe7992 (Dreamstime), Colicaranica (Dreamstime), Dmytro Denysov (Dreamstime), Elad Nussbaum (Dreamstime), Elzeva (Dreamstime), Eva Bocek (Dreamstime), Kasienka (Dreamstime), Lifeontheside (Dreamstime), Maumyhata (Dreamstime), Melissastover (Dreamstime), Micaela Grace Sanna, Minyun Zhou (Dreamstime), Photodynamx (Dreamstime), Rasa Razaniene (Dreamstime), Thomas Oswald (Dreamstime), Yi Li (Dreamstime), Zigf (Dreamstime)

Introduction: Aphinya Photima (Shutterstock), Evgeniya Pashkova (Dreamstime)

Chapter 1: Africa Studio (Shutterstock), bundid vc (Shutterstock), Eric Isselee (Shutterstock), everytime (Shutterstock), Irina Kozorog (Shutterstock), Joanna Zaleska (Shutterstock), Micaela Grace Sanna, milanik (Shutterstock), Nataliya Kuznetsova (Shutterstock), Oleg Gekman (Shutterstock), Tsekhmister (Shutterstock), Vladimir Wrangel (Shutterstock), Vladislav T. Jirousek (Shutterstock), vvvita (Shutterstock), Yuri Kravchenko (Shutterstock), Yury Barsukov (Shutterstock)

Chapter 2: Akaphat Porntepkasemsan (Dreamstime), Alena Stalmashonak (Dreamstime), Anton Petukhov (Dreamstime), Axel Bueckert (Dreamstime), Azaliya (Dreamstime), Catalina Zaharescu Tiensuu (Dreamstime), Dadoodas (Dreamstime), Docer (Dreamstime), Elisa Bistocchi (Dreamstime), Irina Kozhemyakina (Dreamstime), Isselee (Dreamstime), Jason Kolenda (Dreamstime), Marcin Winnicki (Dreamstime), Mark Hayes (Dreamstime), Mbenson255 (Dreamstime), Micaela Grace Sanna, Pavel Shabalin (Dreamstime), Sarkao (Dreamstime), Sergioua (Dreamstime), Sonsedskaya (Dreamstime), Syda Productions (Dreamstime), Utekhina Anna (Shutterstock), Vydrin (Dreamstime)

Chapter 3: Elya Vatel (Shutterstock), Ian Allenden (Dreamstime), Mangroove (Dreamstime), Micaela Grace Sanna, Nicolkulish (Dreamstime), Rattoeur (Dreamstime), Steveheap (Dreamstime), Wavebreakmedia Ltd (Dreamstime)

Chapter 4: Adogslifephoto (Dreamstime), Anatoliy Gagarinov (Dreamstime), Anna Yakimova (Dreamstime), Bogdan Carstina (Dreamstime), , Davidtb (Dreamstime), Deyangeorgiev (Dreamstime), Dragonika (Dreamstime), Evgeniya Tiplyashina (Dreamstime), Ian Andreiev (Dreamstime), Igor Zhorov (Dreamstime), Kateryna Dyellalova (Dreamstime), Lio2012 (Dreamstime), Marilyn Gould (Dreamstime), Micaela Grace Sanna, Nedim Bajramovic (Dreamstime), Peter Wollinga (Dreamstime), Pimmimemom (Dreamstime), Ramonespelt (Dreamstime), Sarah-jane Allen (Dreamstime), Sergey Taran (Dreamstime), Studiobarcelona (Dreamstime), Ufuk Uyanik (Dreamstime)

Pages 59–62: Andreea Dobrescu (Dreamstime), Anna Yakimova (Dreamstime), Arenaphotouk (Dreamstime), Brett Critchley (Dreamstime), Christophher Lewis (Dreamstime), David Lloyd (Dreamstime), Dmytro Denysov (Dreamstime), Eclypse78 (Dreamstime), Ekaterina Kokushkina (Dreamstime), Elya Vatel (Shutterstock), Halil I. Inci (Dreamstime), Hellem (Dreamstime), Iluvatar (Dreamstime), Leonardo Viti (Shutterstock), Miaufoto (Dreamstime), Micaela Grace Sanna, Misscanon (Dreamstime), Mylaphotography (Dreamstime), Natalia Bratslavsky (Dreamstime), Sarah-jane Allen (Dreamstime), Socrates (Dreamstime), Sonatik (Dreamstime), Tanyashir (Dreamstime), Tijs Zwinkels (Dreamstime), Tony Campbell (Dreamstime), Wenzhi Lu (Dreamstime)

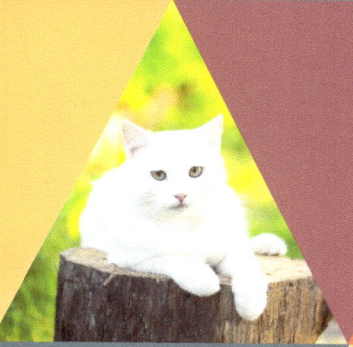

www.ingramcontent.com/pod-product-compliance
Lightning Source LLC
Chambersburg PA
CBHW060813090426
42737CB00002B/48

* 9 7 8 1 6 2 5 2 4 4 5 0 5 *